POPULAR

PIANO

AND KEYBOARDS

PLAYER ZONE ➤ Grade 3

A *Rockschool* Publication

Broomfield House, Broomfield Road, Richmond, Surrey TW9 3HS

Welcome To *Popular Piano* Grade 3

Welcome to the Rockschool *Popular Piano and Electronic Keyboards* Grade 3 pack. This pack contains everything you need to play popular piano in this grade. In the book you will find the exam scores in standard notation with fingering suggestions. The CD features performances of the tunes (with no digital edits) to help you learn the pieces. There are also ten practice ear tests. Handy tips on playing the pieces and the marking schemes can be found in the Guru's Guide on page 21. If you have any queries about this or any other Rockschool exam, please call us on **020 8332 6303** or email us at **office@rockschool.co.uk** or visit our website **http://www.rockschool.co.uk**. Good luck!

Player Zone Techniques in Grade 2 and Grade 3

The eight Rockschool grades are divided into four Zones. *Popular Piano and Electronic Keyboards* Grade 3, along with Grade 2, is part of the *Player Zone.* This Zone is for those of you who are building on key skills to express your musical personality across a range of styles.

Grade 2: in this grade you are beginning to acquire a range of physical and expressive techniques including the use of simple counterpoint, open and closed shell positions, simple voice leading and four in a bar triads in the left hand. You will have the ability to use a range of dynamics and play with basic legato and staccato feels as well as basic use of the sustain pedal.

Grade 3: this grade continues the foundation work laid in the in the previous grade. You will be encountering syncopated semiquavers, swing quavers and quaver triplets as well as a range of time signatures including 6/8. You will be developing your appreciation of style.

Player Zone Popular Piano and Electronic Keyboards Exams at Grade 3

There are **two** types of exam that can be taken using this pack: Grade Exam and Performance Certificate.

• *Popular Piano and Electronic Keyboards* Grade 3 Exam: this is for players who want to develop performance and technical skills

Players wishing to enter for a *Popular Piano and Electronic Keyboards* Grade 3 exam need to prepare **three** pieces, of which **one** may be a free choice piece chosen from outside the printed repertoire. In addition, you must prepare the technical exercises in this book, undetake either a sight reading test or an improvisation & interpretation test, take an ear test and answer general musicianship questions. Samples of these are printed in the books.

• *Player Zone* Performance Certificate in Popular Piano and Electronic Keyboards: this is for players who want to focus on performing in a range of styles

To enter for your *Player Zone* Performance Certificate you play pieces only. You can choose any **five** of the six tunes printed in this book, or you can bring in up to **two** free choice pieces as long as they meet the standards set out in the Guru's Guide on page 21.

Instrument specification and performances in the exam

Candidates bringing in their own instrument must ensure that their keyboard is suitable for the technical requirements of the grade. Electronic keyboards should conform to the following specification: 5 octave keyboard (touch sensitive), keyboard stand, amplification (if required), sustain pedal and all relevant audio and power leads. Keyboards should have a 'realistic' acoustic piano sound which must be used for performance in the exam.

Music Notation Explained

THE MUSICAL STAVE shows pitches and rhythms and is divided by lines into bars. Pitches are named after the first seven letters of the alphabet.

Definitions For Special Piano Notation

Grace Note: Play the grace note on or before the beat depending on the style of music, then move quickly to the note it leads onto.

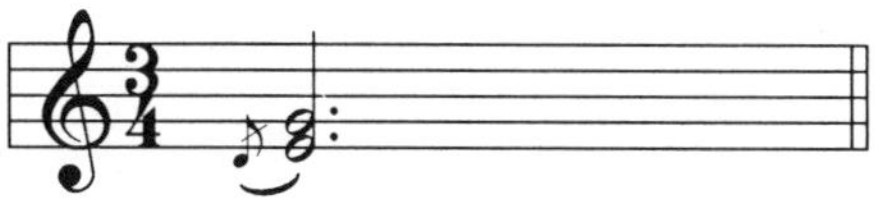

Pedal Marking: Depress and then release the sustain pedal.

Spread Chord: Play the chord from the bottom note up, with the top note being reached by the appropriate notated bar position.

Glissando: Play the notes before the beat as smoothly as possible.

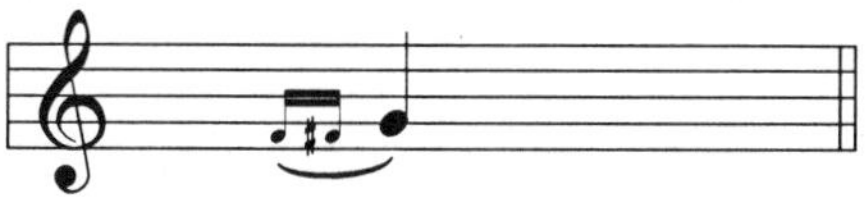

Tremolando: Oscillate at speed between marked notes.

Finger Markings: These numbers represent your fingers. 1 is the thumb, 2 the index finger and so on.

 (accent) • Accentuate note (play it louder).

 (accent) • Accentuate note with great intensity.

 (staccato) • Shorten time value of note.

 (accent) • Accentuate note with more arm weight.

D.%. al Coda • Go back to the sign (%), then play until the bar marked ***To Coda*** ⊕ then skip to the section marked ⊕ ***Coda***.

D.C. al Fine • Go back to the beginning of the song and play until the bar marked ***Fine*** (end).

Una Corda • Use damper (soft) pedal

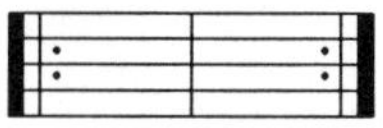 • Repeat bars between signs.

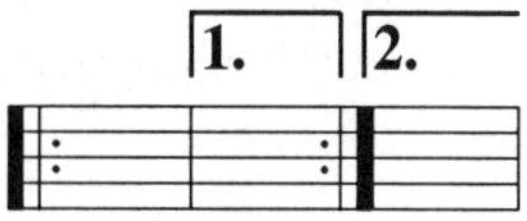

• When a repeated section has different endings, play the first ending only the first time and the second ending only the second time.

Timbo's Gumbo

Tim Richards

rit.

Jumpin' The Barrel

Terry Seabrook

so wrong,
Oo
'cause you're not where you be - long;
Oo)
To Coda
A♭9 D♭ B♭m A♭/C D♭ A♭7/F G♭maj7
in - side my arms.
Bum bum bum bum bum bum bum bum.
Bum bum bum bum bum bum.
B♭m/F B♭m
Verse:
A♭/C D♭ D♭add2/F D♭/F
Bum bum bum bum bum bum.
3. I still be-lieve in sum-mer days. The sea-sons al - ways
G♭ B♭m/F B♭m B♭m7 A♭/C D♭
change and life will find a way.
I'll be your har - ves - ter of

unis.
light and send it out to-night so we can start a-gain. Is love a-
Gb
Absus4
Dbadd2
D.S. 𝄋 al Coda
live? Is love a - live? Is love a - live?
Coda
Db
Bbm
unis.
Ab/C
Db
Dbadd2/F Db/F Gb
Bbm/F Bbm
arms. This is my win-ter song to you. The storm is com-ing soon; it rolls in from the
Bbm7
Ab/C
Db
Dbadd2/F Db/F Gb
Bbm/F Bbm
sea. My love, a bea-con in the night. My words will be your light to car-ry you to

mf
p
mf
mp
mf
f
mp

On A Sentimental Journey

Adrian York

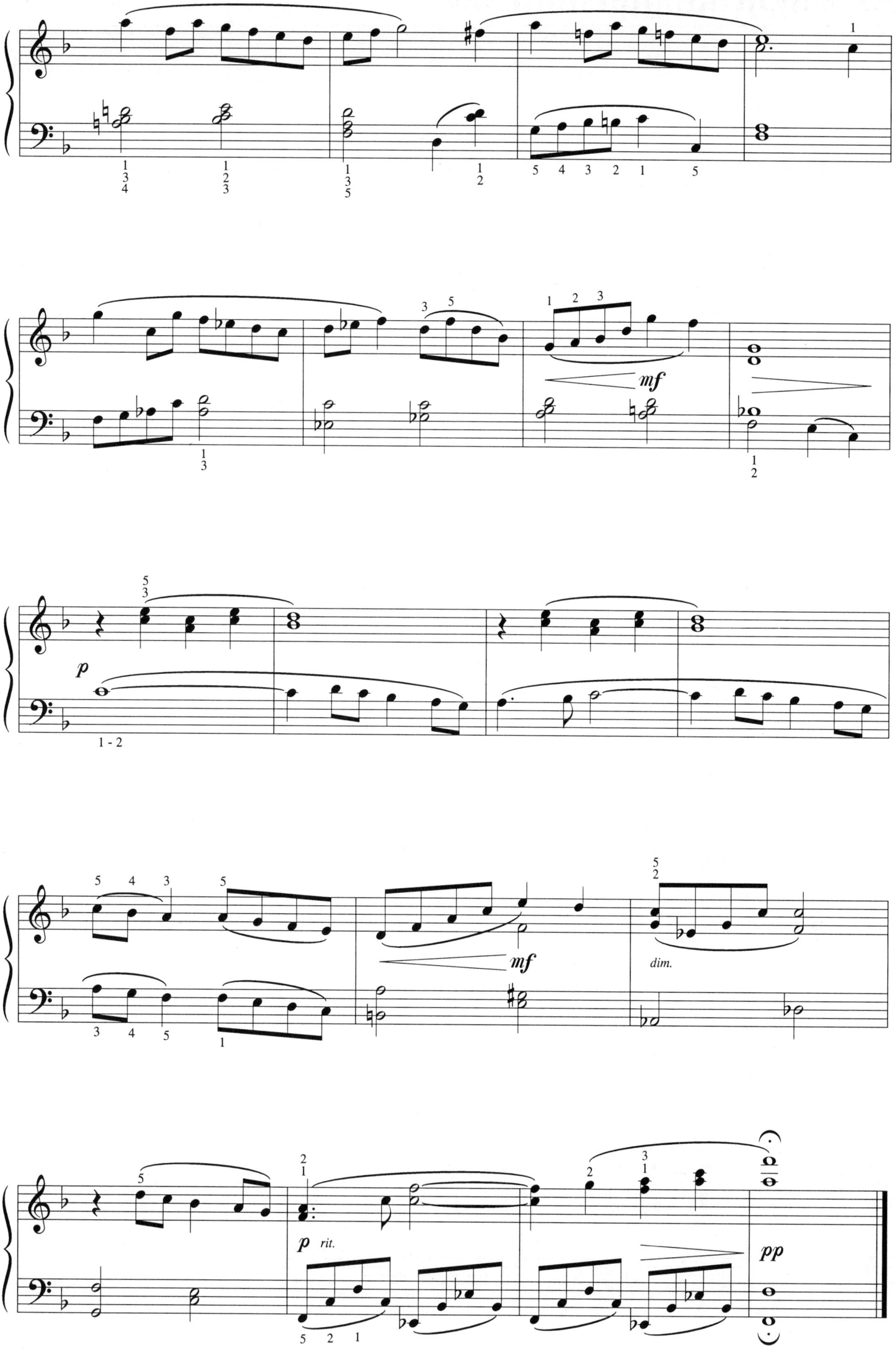
mf
p
mf
dim.
p rit.
pp

Everybody Shout

Alastair Gavin

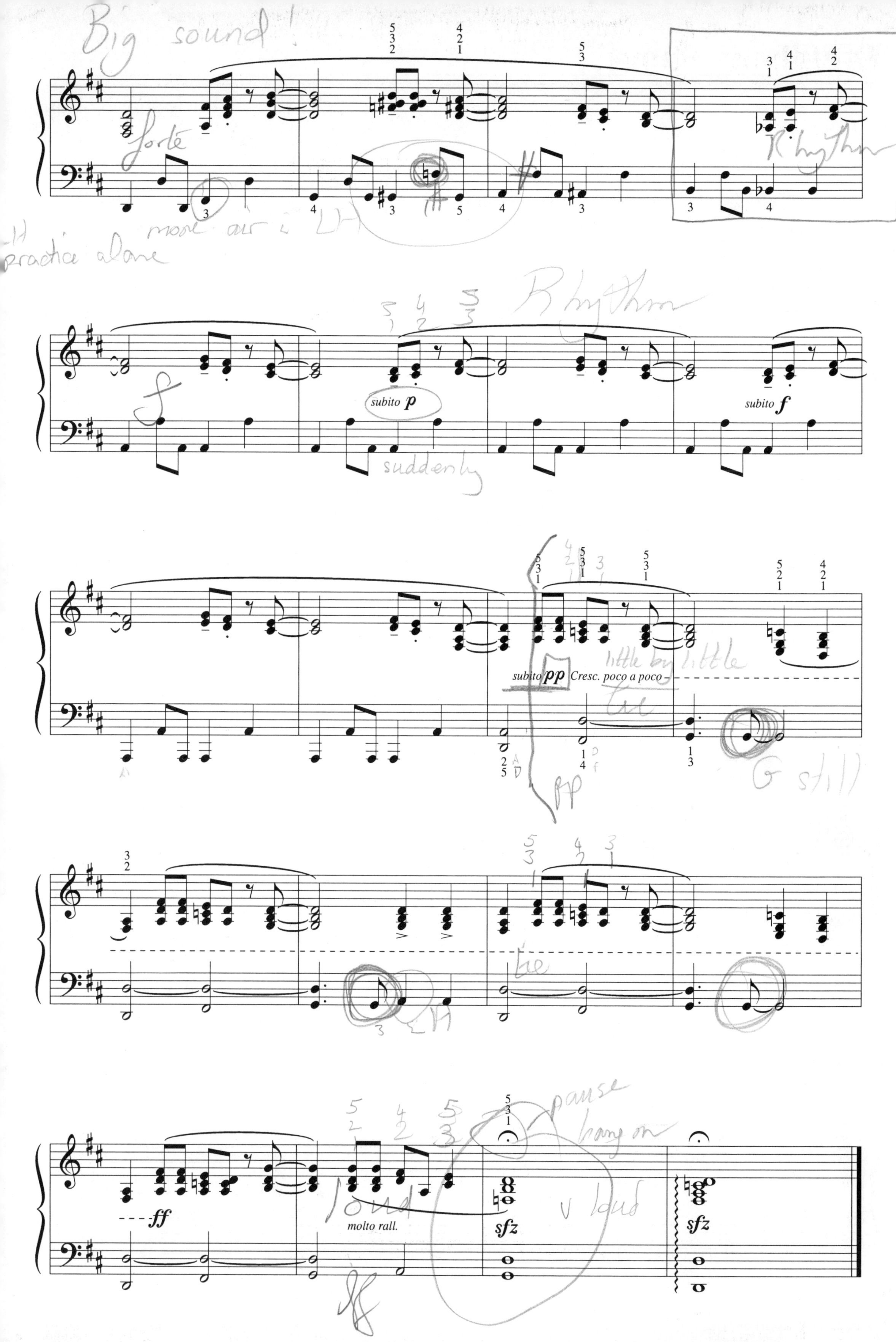
subito p
subito f
subito pp Cresc. poco a poco
ff
molto rall.
sfz
sfz

Tango

Christopher Norton

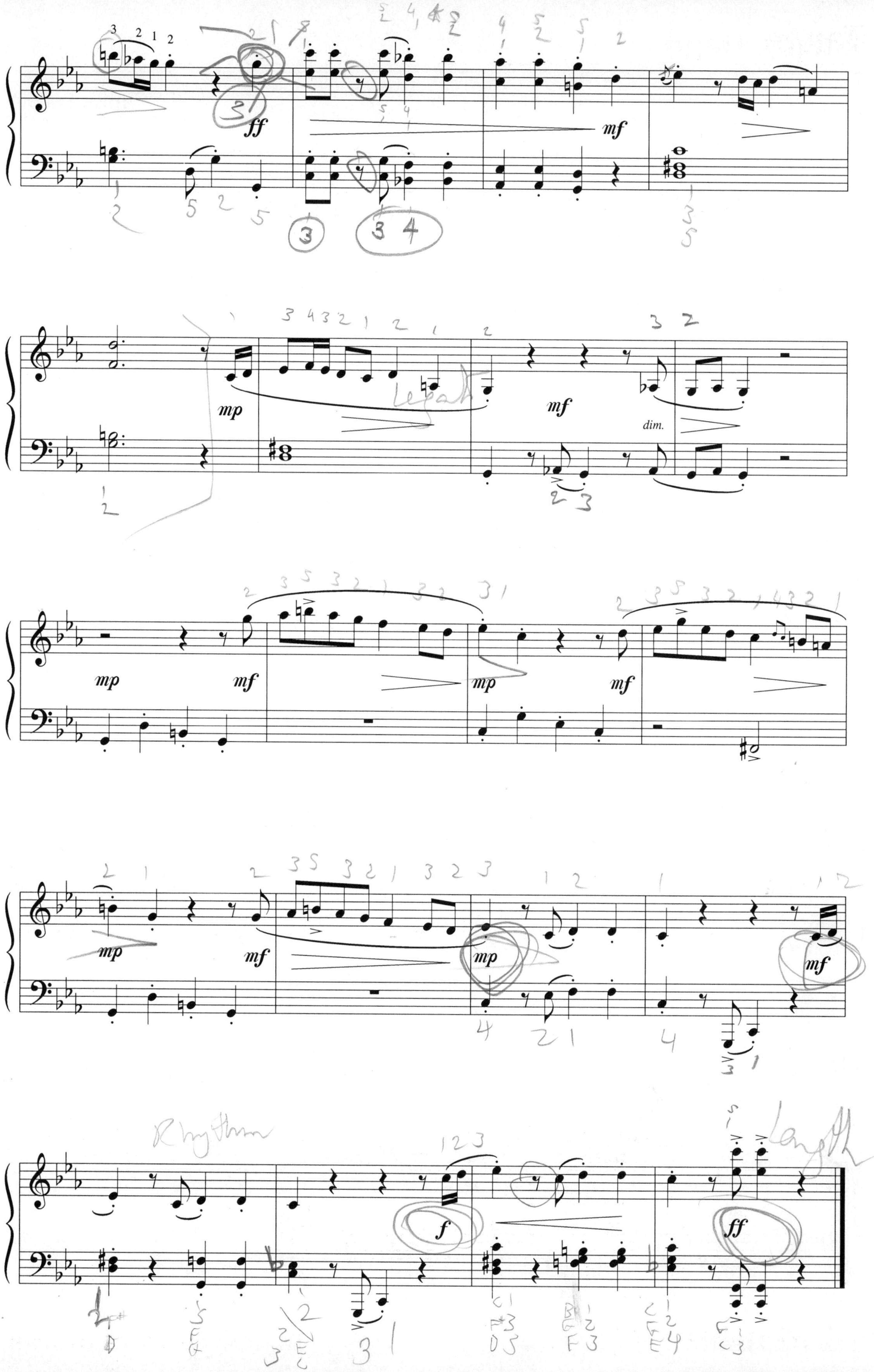
ff
mf
mp
mf
dim.
mp
mf
mp
mf
mp
mf
mp
mf
f
ff

Bozo's Dead

John Eacott

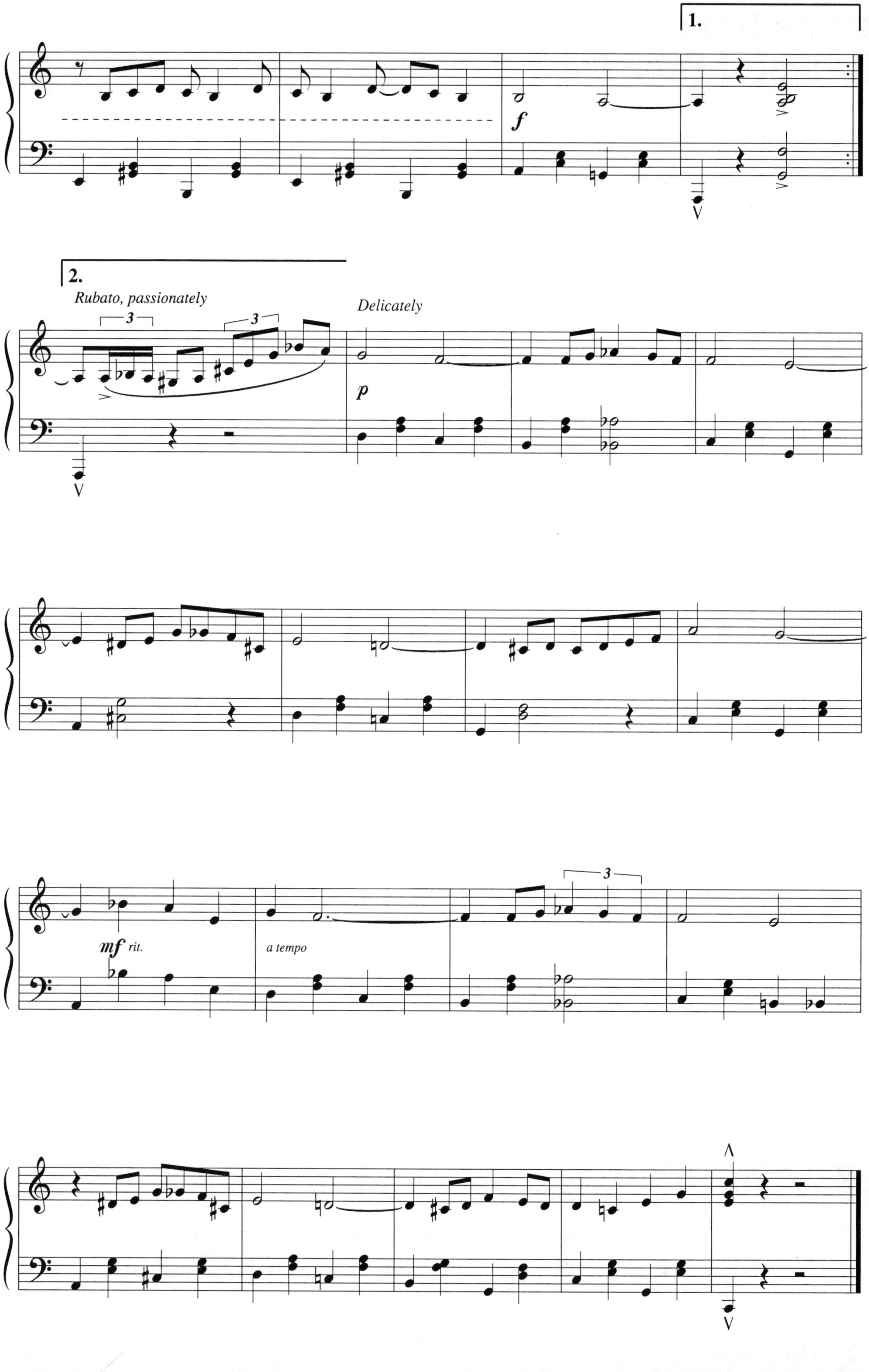
1.
f
2.
Rubato, passionately
3
3
Delicately
p
3
mf rit.
a tempo

Technical Exercises

In this section, the examiner will ask you to play a selection of exercises drawn from each of the two groups shown below. These exercises contain examples of the kinds of scales and arpeggios you can use when playing the pieces. You do not need to memorise the exercises (and can use the book in the exam) but the examiner will be looking for the speed of your response. The examiner will also give credit for the level of your musicality. All exercises should be prepared hands together ascending and descending in the keys and octaves specified except for the pentatonic, chromatic and blues scales, and the arpeggios which should be played hands separately. The fingerings shown below are suggestions only.

The exercises should be played ascending and descending as shown at ♩=90 in either a straight or swung feel as requested by the examiner.

Group A: Scales

D Major Scale

A Mixolydian Scale

C Aeolian Scale

G Dorian Scale

B♭ Lydian Scale

F Major Pentatonic - Right Hand

F Major Pentatonic - Left Hand

C Minor Pentatonic Scale - Right Hand

C Minor Pentatonic Scale - Left Hand

C Blues Scale - Right Hand

C Blues Scale - Left Hand

C Chromatic Scale - Right Hand (2 Octaves, 1 shown)

C Chromatic Scale - Left Hand (2 Octaves, 1 shown)

Group B: Arpeggios

F Major Arpeggio - Right Hand

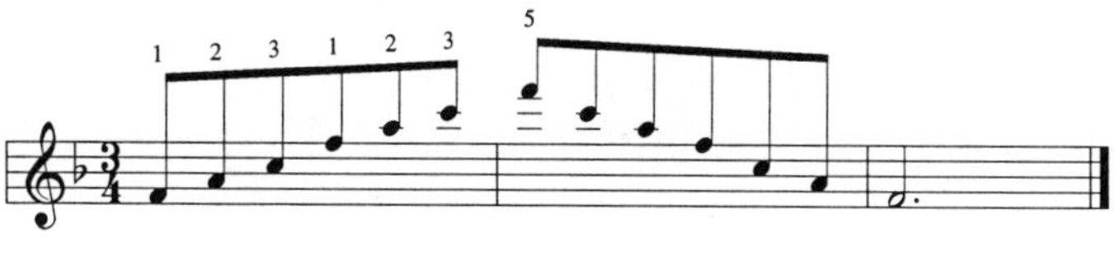

F Major Arpeggio - Left Hand

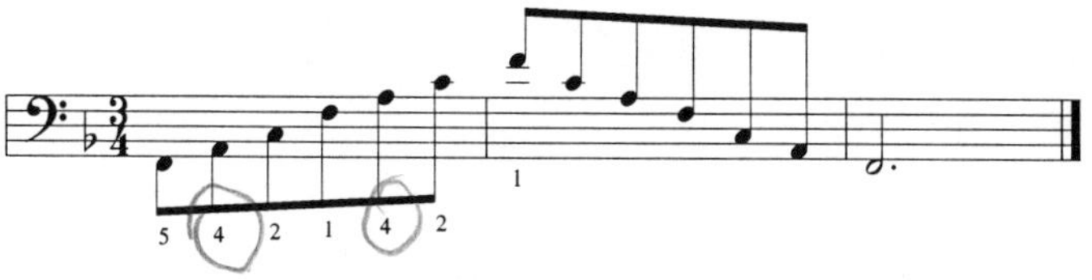

E♭ Minor Arpeggio - Right Hand

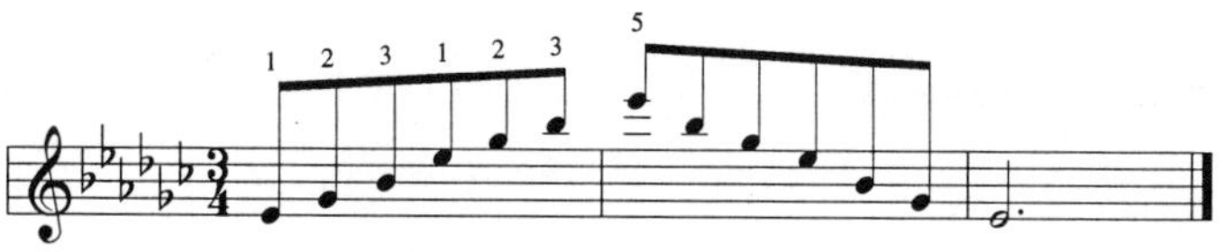

E♭ Minor Arpeggio - Left Hand

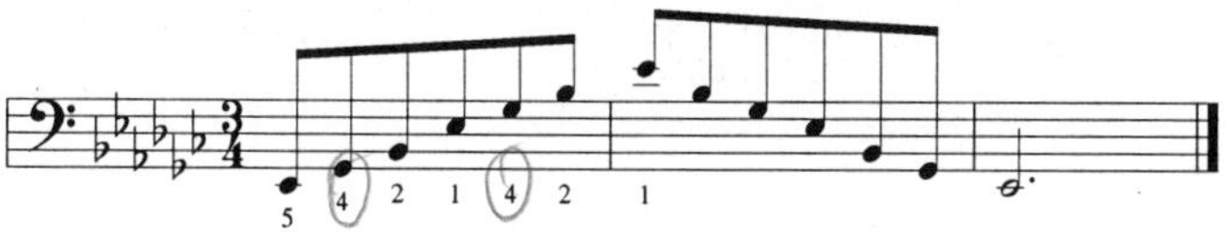

Sight Reading *or* Improvisation & Interpretation

In this section you have a choice between either a sight reading test or an improvisation & interpretation test. Printed below is an example of the type of **sight reading** test you are likely to excounter in the exam. The piece will be composed in the style of one of the six performance pieces. The examiner will allow you 90 seconds to prepare it and will set the tempo for you on a metronome.

Printed below is an example of the type of **improvisation & interpretation** test you are likely to encounter in an exam. You will be asked to play an improvised part based on a chord chart in the style of one of the six performance pieces. The examiner will allow you 90 seconds to prepare it and will set the tempo for you on a metronome.

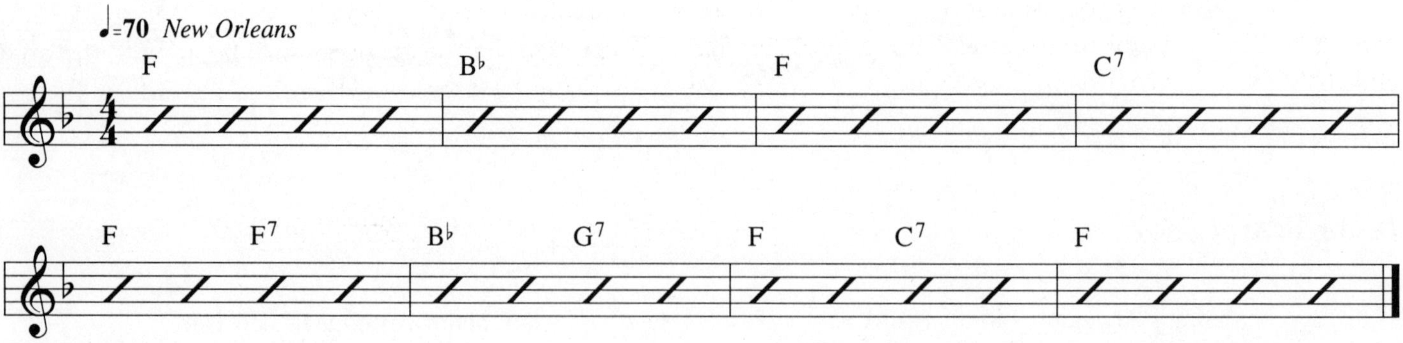

Ear Tests

You will find two ear tests in this grade. The examiner will play each test to you twice on CD. You will find ten examples of the type of test you will get in the exam printed below.

Test 1 (CD Tracks 7 to 11)

You will be asked to play back on your piano/electronic keyboard a simple melody of not more than four bars consisting of notes from one of the following scales: C major, F major, C minor or F minor pentatonic scales. You will be given the key and the first note by the examiner and you will hear the sequence twice.

a) 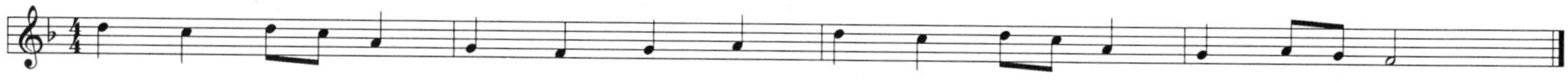

b) 

c) 

d) 

e) 

Test 2 (CD Tracks 12 to 16)

You will be asked to recognise a four chord sequence using chords from the following: I, IV, and V in the keys of either C major, G major or A minor. The examiner will tell you the key and the sequence will begin with the tonic chord. You will hear the sequence twice and may use your piano/electronic keyboard as a guide while the sequence is playing.

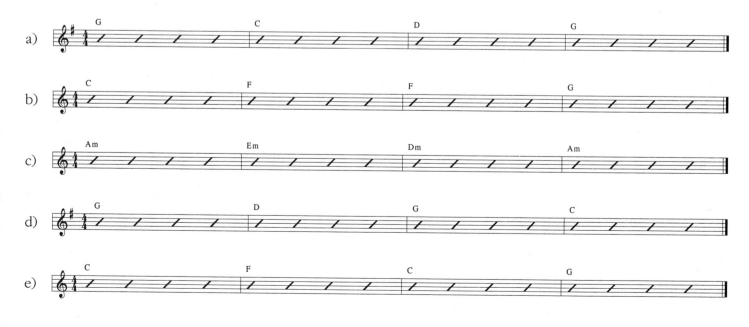

a) 

b) 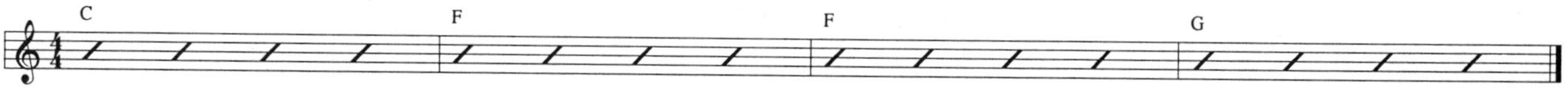

c) 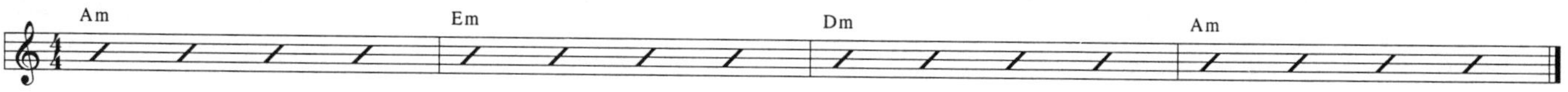

d) 

e) 

General Musicianship Questions

You will be asked five General Musicianship Questions at the end of the exam.

Topics:

i) Music theory
ii) Knowledge of your instrument

The music theory questions will cover the following topics at this grade:

Recognition of pitches	Dynamic Markings (***p***, ***mp***, ***mf***, ***f*** and ***ff***)
Note Values	Cresc. and Dim. plus hairpins
Rests	Accents, staccato and legato
Time Signatures	Repeat Markings
Key Signatures	Grace Notes
Pedal Markings	Fermata (Pause)
Rit. Rall. a tempo, subito,	
simile, molto and poco a poco	

Knowledge of the construction of the following chord types in the keys of the pieces played by you in the exam. Tonic (chord I) only.

Major	(Root position)
Minor	(Root position)
Dominant 7th	(Root position)
Major 7th	(Root position)
Minor 7th	(Root position)
Minor 7♭5	(Root position)

The instrument knowledge questions will cover the following topics at this grade:

Function and use of sustain and damper pedals
Plugging into the amplifier and keyboard (electronic keyboard only)
Correct unplugging procedure (electronic keyboard only)
Volume and tone adjustments on the keyboard (electronic keyboard only)
Appropriate choice of sound (electronic keyboard only)

Knowledge of basic differences between acoustic and electric pianos, synthesizer and electric organ

Questions on all these topics will be based on pieces played by you in the exam

The Guru's Guide To *Popular Piano* Grade 3

This section contains some handy hints compiled by Rockschool's Popular Piano and Keyboards Guru to help you get the most out of the performance pieces. Do feel free to adapt the tunes to suit your playing style. Remember, these tunes are your chance to show your musical imagination and personality.

Fingerings are suggestions only, so use whichever suit your hands best. Please also note that in tunes with optional solo sections, if the solo option is not taken you should move straight onto the next section.

Popular Piano and Electronic Keyboards Grade 3 Tunes

Rockschool tunes help you play in all the popular piano/keyboard styles you enjoy. The pieces have been written or arranged by top performers and composers according to style specifications drawn up by Rockschool.

Each tune printed here falls into one of six categories: blues, jazz, classic, pop/rock, world and film music. These cover roots, contemporary and global styles that influence every generation of performers.

CD track 1 *Blues* ***Timbo's Gumbo***

The left hand of this piece is based on a rumba rhythm, frequently used by the great New Orleans pianist Professor Longhair. It must be solid throughout. Make sure that the middle note of the left hand pattern is always between the second and third beats of the bar. Watch out for the articulation in the right hand.

Composer: Tim Richards. Tim Richards first encountered a piano at the age of eight in a dentist's waiting room. Since then he has become an acclaimed jazz and blues pianist, band leader, composer and educator. His groups include Spirit Level, The Tim Richards Trio and Great Spirit. He performs with blues artists including Otis Grand and Dana Gillespie. He is also known for his widely respected book *Improvising Blues Piano* (Schott & Co).

CD track 2 *Jazz* ***Jumpin' The Barrel***

Using elements of the jump jive, boogie woogie and barrelhouse styles, this minor/major blues needs to be played with a hard swinging quaver feel. Take care over the dynamics, the articulation of the grace notes and accents, and keep a steady pulse.

Composer: Terry Seabrook. Terry writes music regularly for television, animated films and adverts. He records and performs with his own Latin group Cubana Bop on the international Jazz and Latin circuit. He also tutors piano as part of the world famous Jamey Aebersold Summer School each year.

CD track 3 *Classic* ***On A Sentimental Journey***

The performance of this tune can be played with a little rubato (free with the tempo) and must not be too wooden. The right hand melody needs to sing out and when the left hand takes over melodic duties in bar 25 take care to play with enough weight to produce a beautiful tone. Careful pedalling is required for clarity.

Composer: Adrian York. Adrian is Rockschool's piano syllabus director. He is a successful media composer and a fixture on both the jazz and session circuit who has backed many top artists. Rumour has it that a long time ago he used to play in a well known boy band.

CD track 4 *Pop/Rock* ***Everybody Shout***

This piece is similar in feel to Billy Taylor's version of *I Wish*, the theme music to Jonathan Ross's BBC Film Review programme. The secret is the way in which the right hand syncopation sits against the steady left hand rhythm. As well as rhythmic strength, the right hand must have good articulation with the staccatos standing out.

Composer: Alastair Gavin. Alastair has a thriving career as a media composer and is renowned as a fine pianist and keyboardist. He was the keyboard player in the BBC *Rock School* television series in the 1980's and has made appearances with artists as diverse as the Michael Nyman Band, Mari Wilson and trumpeter Harry Beckett.

CD track 5 *World* ***Tango***

This tune has to be performed with a certain panache and sensuality just like the dance itself. Focus on the dynamics, accents and crisp articulation to achieve this.

Composer: Christopher Norton. Christopher has a thriving career composing music for film and television and as a record producer. He is probably best known for his ground breaking *Micro Jazz* series of music education books. ©Boosey and Hawkes Music Publishers Ltd. Reproduced by permission.

CD track 6 *Film* ***Bozo's Dead***

Don't allow yourself to get carried away by the momentum of the tempo changes which need to be controlled whilst appearing to be out of control! Make sure that the left hand offbeat is strong and most importantly let your enjoyment of this piece shine through in the performance.

Composer: John Eacott. John worked through the 80's and 90's with artists as diverse as Roman Holliday, Test Department, Loose Tubes and Goldie. He now has a successful career writing music for film, theatre and television as well as researching into 'generative composition'.

CD Pianist: David Rees-Williams. David has a dual career as a performer and educator. He teaches at Canterbury Christchurch University College and he works internationally as a performer at concerts and festivals, playing everything from baroque harpsichord to jazz piano.

Grade Exam Marking Scheme

The table below shows the marking scheme for the *Popular Piano and Electronic Keyboards* Grade 3 exam.

ELEMENT	PASS	MERIT	DISTINCTION
Piece 1 Piece 2 Piece 3	13 out of 20 13 out of 20 13 out of 20	15 out of 20 15 out of 20 15 out of 20	17+ out of 20 17+ out of 20 17+ out of 20
Technical Exercises	11 out of 15	12 out of 15	13+ out of 15
Either: Sight Reading ***Or:*** Improvisation & Interpretation	6 out of 10	7 out of 10	8+ out of 10
Ear Tests	6 out of 10	7 out of 10	8+ out of 10
General Musicianship Questions	3 out of 5	4 out of 5	5 out of 5
Total Marks	**Pass: 65% +**	**Pass: 75% +**	**Pass: 85% +**

Player Zone Performance Certificate Marking Scheme

The table below shows the marking scheme for the *Player Zone* Performance Certificate. You will see that the Pass mark is now **70%**. The Merit mark is **80%** and the mark for a Distinction performance is **90%**.

ELEMENT	PASS	MERIT	DISTINCTION
Piece 1	14 out of 20	16 out of 20	18+ out of 20
Piece 2	14 out of 20	16 out of 20	18+ out of 20
Piece 3	14 out of 20	16 out of 20	18+ out of 20
Piece 4	14 out of 20	16 out of 20	18+ out of 20
Piece 5	14 out of 20	16 out of 20	18+ out of 20
Total Marks	**Pass: 70% +**	**Merit: 80% +**	**Distinction: 90% +**

Free Choice Song Criteria

You can bring in your own performance pieces to play in any of the exams featured. In the Grade Exams you can bring in **one** piece.

In the *Player Zone* Performance Certificate you may bring in up to **two** pieces. You should read the following criteria carefully.

- Players may bring in either their own compositions or songs already in the public domain, including hits from the charts.
- Songs must be performed solo.
- Players should bring in two copies of the piece to be performed, notated either in standard notation, or chord charts. Players must use an original copy of the tune to be performed, and must provide a second copy for the examiner, which may be a photocopy. For copyright reasons, photocopies handed to the examiner will be retained and destroyed by Rockschool in due course.
- Players may perform either complete songs or extracts: such as a solo part.
- Players should aim to keep their free choice songs below 3 minutes in length.
- Players should aim to make each free choice song of a technical standard similar to those published in the Rockschool *Popular Piano and Electronic Keyboards* Grade 3 book. However, examiners will be awarding credit for how well you perform the song. In general players should aim to play songs that mix the following physical and expressive techniques and rhythm skills:

Physical Techniques: accurate left and right hand co-ordination, stride and barrelhouse left hand patterns, simple New Orleans stylings, two note licks in right hand with static top line plus use of syncopated quaver and semiquaver feels.

Expressive Techniques: legato and staccato, dynamics, accented notes, glissando, a range of grace notes and trills.

Rhythm Skills: songs should contain a mixture of semibreves, minims, crotchets, quavers, semiquavers, swung quavers and shuffle blues patterns, a range of time signatures, tempos and styles.

You, or your teacher, may wish to adapt an existing piece of music to suit the criteria above. You should ensure that any changes to the music are clearly marked on the sheet submitted to the examiner.

Entering Rockschool Exams

Entering a Rockschool exam is easy, whether for the Grade or the *Player Zone* Performance Certificate. Please read through these instructions carefully before filling in the exam entry form. Information on current exam fees can be obtained from Rock School by ringing **020 8332 6303**

- You should enter for the exam of your choice when you feel ready.

- You can enter for any one of three examination periods. These are shown below with their closing dates.

PERIOD	DURATION	CLOSING DATE
Period A	1st February to 15th March	1st December
Period B	15th May to 31st July	1st April
Period C	1st November to 15th December	1st October

These dates will apply from 1st January 2001 until further notice

- Please fill in the form giving your name, address and phone number. Please tick the type and level of exam, along with the period and year. Finally, fill in the fee box with the appropriate amount. You should send this form with a cheque or postal order to: **Rockschool, Broomfield House, 10 Broomfield Road, Richmond, Surrey TW9 3HS.**

- Rockschool will allocate your entry to a centre closest to your postcode and you will receive notification of the exam, showing a date, location and time as well as advice of what to bring to the centre.

- You should inform Rockschool of any cancellations or alterations to the schedule as soon as you can as it is not possible to transfer entries from one centre, or one period, to another without the payment of an administration fee.

- Please bring your music book to the exam. You may not use photocopied music, nor the music used by someone else in another exam. The examiner will stamp each book after each session. Performers may be barred from taking an exam if they use music not otherwise belonging to them.

- You should aim to arrive for your *Popular Piano and Electronic Keyboards* Grade 3 exam fifteen minutes before the time stated on the schedule.

- The exam centre will have a waiting area which you may use prior to being called into the main exam room.

- Each *Popular Piano and Electronic Keyboards* Grade 3 exam is scheduled to last for 25 minutes. You can use a small proportion of this time to get ready.

- About 2 to 3 weeks after the exam you will receive a typed copy of the examiner's mark sheet. Every successful player will receive a Rockschool certificate of achievement.

- Rockschool may defer your entry to the next available exam period if the minimum number of candidates for your local centre is not met.

- For all up to date information refer to the Rockschool website **http://www.rockschool.co.uk**.